WHO LIVES IN THE RAINFOREST?

Susan Canizares • Mary Reid

SCHOLASTIC INC.

NEW YORK · TORONTO · LONDON · AUCKLAND · SYDNEY

Acknowledgments

Science Consultants: Patrick R. Thomas, Ph.D., Bronx Zoo/Wildlife Conservation Park; Glenn Phillips, The New York Botanical Garden; **Literacy Specialist:** Maria Utefsky, Reading Recovery Coordinator, District 2, New York City

Design: MKR Design, Inc.

Photo Research: Barbara Scott

Endnotes: Susan Russell

Photographs: **Cover & p. 1**: Kevin Schafer; p. 2: Alan D. Carey/Photo Researchers, Inc.; p. 3: Marian Bacon/Animals, Animals; p. 4: Tom & Pat Leeson/Photo Researchers, Inc.; p. 5: Robert A. Lubeck/Animals, Animals; p. 6: Michael Fogden/DRK Photo; p. 7: Tom Brakefield/DRK Photo; p. 8: Michael & Patricia Fogden; p. 9: Kevin Schafer; p. 10: Staffan Widstrand/The Wildlife Collection; p. 11: Michael Fogden/DRK Photo; p. 12: Dr. Nigel Smith/Animals, Animals.

Library of Congress Cataloging-in-Publication Data
Canizares, Susan, 1960-
Who lives in the rainforest? / Susan Canizares, Mary Reid.
p. cm. -- (Science emergent readers)
"Scholastic early childhood."
Includes index.
Summary: Photographs and simple text explore the variety of animals found in the Amazon rainforest.
ISBN 0-590-76961-8 (pbk.: alk. paper)
1. Rain forest animals--Juvenile literature. [1. Rain forests. animals]
I. Reid, Mary. II. Title. III. Series.
QL112.C35 1998
591.734--dc21   97-34202
                                                                                     CIP AC

20 19 18 17   03   02

Who lives in the rainforest?

Iguanas do.

Snakes too.

Jaguars do.

Pumas too.

Tamanduas do.

Anteaters too.

Butterflies do.

Toucans too.

Sloths do.

Coatis too.

Could you live in the rainforest?

Who Lives in the Rainforest?

Wildlife is abundant and diverse in a tropical rainforest. Over half the world's species of wildlife can be found there. One of the things that accounts for this richness is the plentiful supply of water, a necessity for all plants and animals. Most of the action happens in the treetops. The Black Howler Monkey (left), who lives high up, is from a family of monkeys that are the noisiest anywhere. Their roars define their clan's territory and can be heard up to a mile away.

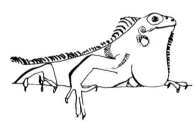

The Iguana (left) looks like a tiny dragon, but in reality it is quite timid. It is herbivorous, an expert climber and swimmer, and can grow to be 6 feet long. The Emerald Boa (right) is easily hidden among the leaves of the trees by its bright green color. Its strong tail wraps firmly around tree trunks while it reaches out to capture its prey: birds and lizards.

The Jaguar (left) and the Puma (right) are the largest cats that live in the rainforest. Jaguars like to hunt reptiles that live around the water. They are also good fishermen and powerful swimmers. Pumas have a wider hunting range and can live in the mountains and on the plains, pursuing sheep, deer, and goats.

The Tamandua (left) is a cousin of the Giant Anteater (right), and although it is not as large, it also has powerful front feet with big claws that are used to tear open ant and termite nests. The tamandua's tail is prehensile, helping it climb trees. The anteater's tail is long and bushy, making a warm blanket when it curls up to sleep.

The Metalmark Butterfly (left) is one of the more than 2,000 species that make up this large and diverse family. Although scientists are not sure why the bill of the Toucan (right) is so large, one job it does is to pull the fruit and berries that are the toucan's food. The bill is both strong and lightweight.

The Three-Toed Sloth (left), like its two-toed cousin, moves in slow motion. Because it eats mostly leaves, it doesn't have to go very far to find dinner. The Coatimundi (right) is a member of the raccoon family and has many of the same habits. It is omnivorous, intelligent, mischievous, and sometimes aggressive.